Questions and Answers: Countries

Iraq

by Kremena Spengler

Consultant:
Reeva S. Simon
Assistant Director, Middle East Institute
Columbia University
New York, New York

Capstone
press

Mankato, Minnesota

Fact Finders is published by Capstone Press
151 Good Counsel Drive, P.O. Box 669, Mankato, Minnesota 56002
www.capstonepress.com

Library of Congress Cataloging-in-Publication Data
Spengler, Kremena.
    Iraq / by Kremena Spengler.
    p. cm.—(Fact finders. Questions and answers: Countries)
    Includes bibliographical references and index.
    ISBN 0-7368-2691-2 (hardcover)
    1. Iraq—Juvenile literature. I. Title. II. Series.
DS70.62.S645 2005
956.7—dc22   2004000449

Summary: A brief introduction to Iraq, following a simple question-and-answer format that
    discusses land features, government, housing, transportation, industries, education,
    sports, art forms, holidays, food, and family life. Includes a map, fast facts, and charts.

Editorial Credits
Megan Schoeneberger, editor; Kia Adams, series designer; Jennifer Bergstrom, book designer;
    maps.com, map illustrator; Wanda Winch, photo researcher; Scott Thoms, photo editor;
    Eric Kudalis, product planning editor

Photo Credits
Alison Keroack, 29 (top, coins); AP Photo/Nasser Nasser, 23; Capstone Press Archives, 29
(top, bill); Corbis/AFP, 25; Corbis/Ed Kashi, 14–15, 26–27; Corbis/Lynsey Addario, 18–19;
Corbis/Michael S. Yamashita, 10–11; Corbis/Nik Wheeler, cover (background);
Corbis/Reuters, 9; Corbis/Reuters NewMedia Inc., 13; Corbis Saba/Shepard Sherbell, 21;
Corel, 1; Getty Images Inc./AFP Photo/Karim Sahib, 17; Getty Images Inc./Hulton Archive,
7; Save the Children UK/Brendan Paddy, cover (foreground); StockHaus Limited, 29
(bottom); SuperStock, 4; U.S. Army/Staff Sgt. Kevin Wastler, 12

Artistic Effects
Photodisc/Siede Preis, 16

1 2 3 4 5 6 09 08 07 06 05 04

Table of Contents

Where is Iraq? 4

When did Iraq become a country? 6

What type of government does Iraq have? 8

What kind of housing does Iraq have? 10

What are Iraq's forms of transportation? 12

What are Iraq's major industries? 14

What is school like in Iraq? 16

What are Iraq's favorite sports and games? 18

What are the traditional art forms in Iraq? 20

What major holidays do people in Iraq celebrate? 22

What are the traditional foods of Iraq? 24

What is family life like in Iraq? 26

Features

Iraq Fast Facts 28

Money and Flag 29

Learn to Speak Arabic 30

Glossary 30

Internet Sites 31

Read More 31

Index 32

Where is Iraq?

Iraq is a country in the Middle East. It is about as large as the U.S. state of California.

Northern Iraq's landforms include mountains. A group of people called the Kurds live in the foothills of the mountains.

The Syrian Desert covers southwestern Iraq. The desert has many dry valleys. Rivers flow in the valleys when rain falls.

Many people live in the area where the Tigris and the Euphrates rivers meet. ➤

4

Map of Iraq

Legend

✪	Capital
•	City
‖‖‖	Desert
⛰	Mountain Range
∿	River

TURKEY

SYRIA

Euphrates River

Tigris River

Mosul

Kirkuk

Tikrit

IRAN

JORDAN

Syrian Desert

Baghdad

I R A Q

SAUDI ARABIA

Basra

KUWAIT

Persian Gulf

N W E S

Scale

0   100   200 Miles

0   100   200 Kilometers

Plains make up the rest of Iraq. Two large
rivers run through the plains. They are
called the Tigris and the Euphrates rivers.
Over thousands of years, these rivers have
flooded and left behind rich soil.

When did Iraq become a country?

People have lived in Iraq for thousands of years. But Iraq did not become a country until 1932. In that year, Iraq won its freedom from Great Britain.

In 1920, the area that is now Iraq came under British control. Britain set the borders of modern Iraq. It also set up Iraq's laws. Britain made Iraq into a **monarchy** led by a king. Faisal I became Iraq's first king. In 1932, Britain's control over Iraq ended.

Fact!

In about 3500 BC, the world's first known civilization, Sumer, began in what is now southeastern Iraq. Sumerians used the world's first written language.

King Faisal I was Iraq's first king.

Kings ruled Iraq until 1958. In that year, Iraq's army took control. In 1979, a **dictator** named Saddam Hussein took over the government. He ruled in Iraq until 2003.

What type of government does Iraq have?

Iraq's government is changing. During Hussein's rule, he had complete control of Iraq. He was the president and **prime minister**. He also was in charge of the army. Hussein led Iraq into many wars. He treated many Iraqis unfairly.

In 2003, the United States led a war to force Hussein from power. Other countries helped in the war. Hussein's rule ended.

Fact!

Saddam Hussein led Iraq into war with Iran in the 1980s. He also tried to invade Iraq's neighbor Kuwait in 1991.

Members of Iraq's governing council helped Iraq form a new government.

مَجلِس الحُكم

U.S. leaders named 25 Iraqis to run Iraq. The council is helping Iraq form a new government. U.S. leaders must agree with the council's choices. In time, Iraqis will vote for their laws and their leaders.

What kind of housing does Iraq have?

Many Iraqi homes are made of brick or **stucco**. They have flat roofs and stone floors. These homes have thick walls. During hot summers, the thick walls keep rooms cool. Even without air conditioners, air stays cooler indoors than it is outdoors.

Where do people in Iraq live?

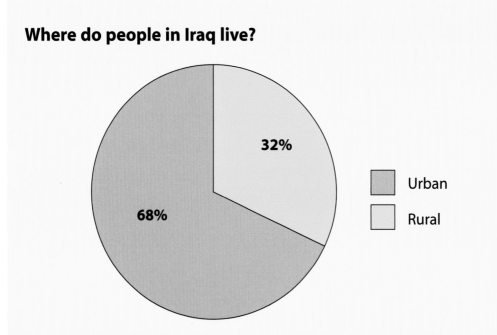

32%

68%

Urban

Rural

Many Iraqis live in houses made of mud or stucco.

Housing is hard to find. War has destroyed many buildings. People are poor. To make more money, **landlords** raise their rent prices. Families who can't pay must leave their homes. Some Iraqis live in empty government buildings. Others live in tents.

What are Iraq's forms of transportation?

Many Iraqis can't afford to buy their own cars. In cities, many people ride bicycles. People use camels, donkeys, taxis, and buses to travel in the countryside.

Iraqis also use railroads to carry goods. The main railroads in Iraq run northwest to southeast. They connect Iraq with Syria, Turkey, and Europe.

Trains between Iraq and other countries began running again in 2003. ➤

An Iraqi family travels on a cart pulled by a donkey.

Iraq has only a few highways. These roads connect the capital, Baghdad, to other cities and countries. Bombs from many wars have destroyed some roads and bridges in Iraq.

What are Iraq's major industries?

Iraq makes most of its money selling oil to other countries. In the 1990s, many countries punished Iraq for attacking Kuwait. They stopped buying oil from Iraq. Later, countries exchanged food and medicine for oil. Today, other countries have begun buying oil from Iraq again.

What does Iraq import and export?

Imports	Exports
food	oil
manufactured products	
medicine	

Workers fix pipes at an Iraqi oil company.

Iraqi farmers grow food and raise animals. The area between the Tigris and Euphrates rivers has rich farmland. Wheat, **barley**, and rice are important crops. Other crops include dates, apples, and grapes. Farmers also raise cattle, sheep, goats, and chickens.

What is school like in Iraq?

Iraqi children must go to school from age 6 to 11. This six-year elementary school is called the first level. First level students learn reading, math, and other subjects.

Between ages 12 and 17, many children go to the second level of school. For the first three years of this level, students study math and science. For the next three years, they study many subjects to prepare for college.

Fact!

The first and second levels of school are free for Iraqi students.

Students in Iraq learn reading, math, and other subjects.

During the 2003 war, many school buildings were damaged. Thieves stole desks, chalkboards, and lightbulbs from the buildings. Many students could not go back to school until their classrooms were repaired.

What are Iraq's favorite sports and games?

Soccer is the favorite sport in Iraq. Many neighborhoods have soccer teams. People enjoy going to games or watching games on TV. In January 2004, Iraqis chose a new national soccer team to compete for the World Cup.

Iraqis also play or watch other sports and games. Some favorite sports are boxing, volleyball, and weight lifting. Chess and backgammon are popular games.

Fact!

Abdel Wahed Aziz won Iraq's only Olympic medal. He received a bronze medal in 1960 for weight lifting.

Soccer is the most popular sport in Iraq.

Iraq's mountains and rivers make outdoor activities popular. Iraqis hike and camp in the mountains. Boating, fishing, and swimming are popular on the rivers.

What are the traditional art forms in Iraq?

Iraq is known for its writers. Many years ago, a person living in what is now Iraq wrote a story about a hero named Gilgamesh. Today, many readers study this famous story. Since the 1930s, Iraqi writers have written many poems and books about the people and government of Iraq.

Fact!

Nazik al-Mala'ika is a famous Iraqi poet. She began writing poetry as a child. For more than 50 years, her poetry has been translated into many languages.

Flower designs are common patterns on Iraqi tiles.

Iraqi painters are well known in the Arab world. Famous painters combine styles from France, Spain, and Russia. Many Iraqi artists use flowers and patterns in their artwork. These images appear on pots, carpets, and tiles.

What major holidays do people in Iraq celebrate?

Most Iraqis are **Muslims** and celebrate holidays of the Islamic religion. The month of Ramadan is one Islamic holiday. Ramadan is the ninth month of the Islamic calendar. During this holy time, adults don't eat or drink between sunrise and sunset. At the end of the month, they celebrate Eid al-Fitr. Muslims feast for three days with family and friends.

What other holidays do people in Iraq celebrate?

Ashoura
Mouloud
New Year's Day
Peace Day

Eid al-Fitr celebrations follow the month of Ramadan.

In 2003, the new government made a new national holiday. The national holiday is celebrated April 9. On this day, forces led by the United States took control of Baghdad. They freed the Iraqi people from Hussein's power.

What are the traditional foods of Iraq?

Most Iraqis eat foods they can grow and raise themselves. Farmers grow wheat, rice, and vegetables. They use the wheat to make flat, round bread. Iraqis also use rice in many meals. They mix rice with vegetables and meat.

Fact!

Iraqi desserts are sweet. Baklava is made of thin sheets of dough layered with honey and nuts. Dates in syrup and date pastries are also popular treats.

An Iraqi woman uses a cloth mold to shape bread dough.

Many Iraqis also eat meat. Lamb, beef, chicken, and fish are popular. Fish comes from the Tigris River. Iraqis grill meat chunks and vegetables on thin sticks to make **kebabs**. Stuffed lamb and meatballs are also common.

What is family life like in Iraq?

Extended families in Iraq often live together. Children, especially in farm areas, live with parents, grandparents on their father's side, uncles, aunts, and cousins. Relatives visit each other often.

What are the ethnic backgrounds of people in Iraq?

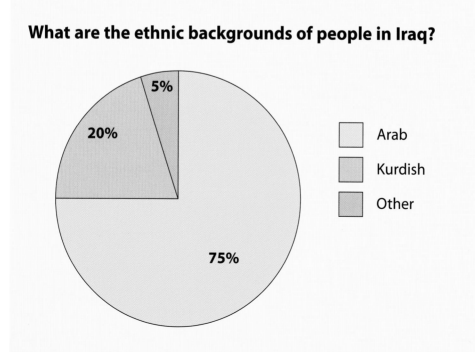

- Arab
- Kurdish
- Other

5%
20%
75%

Iraqi children often help care for younger siblings.

Iraqi parents have different jobs. Fathers usually make most decisions. Mothers care for the children and home. In some families, fathers do the grocery shopping. These men feel that women should not go to a market.

Iraq Fast Facts

Official name:

Republic of Iraq

Land area:

166,858 square miles
(432,162 square kilometers)

Average annual precipitation (Baghdad):

6 inches (15 centimeters)

Average January temperature (Baghdad):

50 degrees Fahrenheit
(10 degrees Celsius)

Average July temperature (Baghdad):

95 degrees Fahrenheit
(35 degrees Celsius)

Population:

24,683,313 people

Capital city:

Baghdad

Languages:

Arabic and Kurdish

Natural resources:

oil

Religions:

Islamic*   97%
  *65% of Iraqis practice a form
    of Islam called Shi'a; 32% practice
    Sunni Islam.

Christian or other   3%

Money and Flag

Money:

Iraq's money is called the new Iraqi dinar. It replaced the old dinar in January 2004. In 2004, 1 U.S. dollar equaled about .3 dinar. One Canadian dollar equaled about .2 dinar.

Flag:

Iraq used the flag shown here until April 2004. It had three equal stripes of red, white, and black. The white stripe had three five-pointed green stars. An Arabic phrase, Allahu Akbar, which means "God Is Great," was written between the stars.

Learn to Speak Arabic

Arabic uses a different alphabet than English. Here are some Arabic words spelled using English letters.

English	Arabic	Pronunciation
hello	marhaba	(MAR-hab-ah)
good-bye	ma'a s-salama	(MAH-ah sah-LAH-mah)
please	min fadlak	(MIHN FAHD-lahk)
thank you	shokran	(show-KRAHN)
yes	aywa	(EYE-wah)
no	laa	(LAH)

Glossary

barley (BAR-lee)—a common type of grain; grains are the seeds of a cereal plant.

dictator (DIK-tay-tur)—someone who has complete control of a country, often ruling it unjustly

kebab (ke-BAHB)—cubes of meat and vegetables held together with a thin stick and grilled

landlord (LAND-lord)—a person who owns and rents out an apartment, a room, a house, or other property

monarchy (MON-ar-kee)—a government led by a king or a queen

Muslim (MUHZ-luhm)—a person who follows the religion of Islam; Islam is a religion whose followers believe in one god, Allah, and that Muhammad is his prophet.

prime minister (PRIME MIN-uh-stur)—the person in charge of a government in some countries; Saddam Hussein was the prime minister of Iraq until 2003.

stucco (STUH-koh)—a mixture of cement, sand, and lime used as a hard covering for walls

Internet Sites

FactHound offers a safe, fun way to find Internet sites related to this book. All of the sites on FactHound have been researched by our staff.

Here's how:
1. Visit *www.facthound.com*
2. Type in this special code **0736826912** for age-appropriate sites. Or enter a search word related to this book for a more general search.
3. Click on the **Fetch It** button.

FactHound will fetch the best sites for you!

Read More

Rivera, Sheila. *Rebuilding Iraq*. War in Iraq. Edina, Minn.: ABDO & Daughters, 2004.

Sapre, Reshma. *Iraq*. Steadwell Books World Tour. Chicago: Raintree, 2003.

Taus-Bolstad, Stacy. *Iraq in Pictures*. Visual Geography Series. Minneapolis: Lerner, 2004.

Walsh, Kieran. *Iraq*. Countries in the News. Vero Beach, Fla.: Rourke, 2004.

Index

agriculture, 15, 24
art forms, 20–21

Baghdad, 13, 23, 28

capital. See Baghdad
climate, 4, 10, 28

education, 16–17
ethnic groups, 26
Euphrates River, 4, 5, 15
exports, 14

Faisal I, King, 6, 7
families, 13, 22, 26–27
farming. See agriculture
flag, 29
foods, 24–25

games, 18
government, 7, 8–9, 23
Great Britain, 6

history, 6–7
holidays, 22–23
housing, 10–11
Hussein, Saddam, 7, 8, 23

imports, 14
industries, 14–15

Kuwait, 8, 14

landforms, 4–5, 19
languages, 6, 28

money, 29

natural resources, 28

oil, 14, 15, 28

population, 10, 28
prime minister, 8

railroads, 12
recreation, 19
religions, 22, 28

schools. See education
sports, 18–19
Sumer, 6
Syrian Desert, 4

Tigris River, 4, 5, 15, 25
transportation, 12–13

wars, 8, 11, 13, 17
weather. See climate